PRIMERS PRIMERS S

ERS PRIMERS PRIMERS PRIM

PRIMERS PRIMERS PRIMERS

ERS PRIMERS PRIMERS PRIM

PRIMERS PRIMERS PRIMERS

ERS PRIMERS PRIMERS PRIM

PRIMERS PRIMERS PRIMERS

Primers
Volume One

Primers
Volume One

Geraldine Clarkson

Maureen Cullen

Katie Griffiths

Lucy Ingrams

Selected by
Kathryn Maris and Jane Commane

Nine
Arches
Press

Primers Volume One
Geraldine Clarkson, Maureen Cullen, Katie Griffiths
and Lucy Ingrams

Selected by Kathryn Maris and Jane Commane

ISBN: 978-1-911027-03-4

Copyright © the individual authors.

Primers logo design by 3 Men and a Suit
www.3men.co.uk

All rights reserved. No part of this work may be reproduced, stored or transmitted in any form or by any means, graphic, electronic, recorded or mechanical, without the prior written permission of the publisher.

The individual authors have asserted their rights under Section 77 of the Copyright, Designs and Patents Act 1988 to be identified as the author of this work.

First published April 2016 by:

Nine Arches Press
PO Box 6269
Rugby
CV21 9NL
United Kingdom

www.ninearchespress.com

Printed in Britain by:

Imprint Digital

www.imprintdigital.com

Primers Volume One
is supported by and produced in partnership with:

About the Editors:

Kathryn Maris is a poet from New York City who now lives in London. She has published two collections (*God Loves You* and *The Book of Jobs*) and a pamphlet, *2008* (If A Leaf Falls Press, 2016). Her poems have appeared in *Granta, Poetry, Ploughshares, The New Statesman, The Pushcart Prize Anthology* and *The Best British Poetry*. She teaches at the Poetry School.

Jane Commane is a poet, editor at Nine Arches Press, and co-editor for *Under the Radar* magazine. Born in Coventry and living in Warwickshire, Jane was recently selected to join the 2016-17 cohort of Writing West Midlands' Room 204 Writer Development Programme. Her poems have featured in *Iota, The Morning Star, And Other Poems, Tears in the Fence, Best British Poetry* and in *Lung Jazz: Young British Poets for Oxfam*.

Contents

Foreword by Julia Bird	11

Geraldine Clarkson

that light	15
Podcarp	17
Camelament	19
Leaving Glawdom by night –	20
Violette, Michaela et al, according to Mildred	22
My Mother, the Monsoon	24
Queen Tamp	25
When we awake	26
Love Cow	27
When tooraloos were taboo,	29
a young woman undressed me and	30
Declare	31

Maureen Cullen

A Case o Fraud	35
Annalise's Stars	36
Revolving Door	37
New Shoes	38
On Two Wheels	39
Owl	40
Apprentice	41
Wee Wifie	42
Scots Rose	43
Dreaming Mum	44
Milk Tooth	45
The Sisters	46
Strangers	47
The Thin Place	48
Saumon	49
The Gloamin	50

Katie Griffiths

Capo	53
The Friends You Keep	54
The Road to Split	55
The Knight of Swords	56
A Lack of Minarets	57
Dashboard	59
The Urbane Terrorist	61
Leaving	62
A Haircut for Radovan Karadžić Before the International War Crimes Tribunal	63
A Village Priest and I Watch the Solar Eclipse Through the Safety of a Kitchen Colander	64
Tips for a Post-War Correspondent	65
Soil	67
I Waved my Placard	68
Words for Sorrow	69

Lucy Ingrams

Signs	73
June	74
A hearting space	75
So will there be apples?	77
August letter	79
Slow air	80
Stonechat's song	81
Leaf litter	82
Snow tide	83
In the half light,	84
Pinkfoots	85
Spate	86
Some things starlings are sensitive to:	87
Blue hour	88

Acknowledgements	91

Foreword

What a volume you hold in your hands! The Poetry School is incredibly excited to be associated with it. As an organisation, we are dedicated to fostering the skills of poets of all levels – from beginners attending their first workshop to experienced writers finding their own readership. Primers is our first big project in a long time which has helped new poets' work into print, and we are very pleased to have forged the relationship with Nine Arches Press which enables this to happen.

Even if you work in the arts and it says 'poetry' on your business cards, the office-based intricacies of a project such as Primers are mostly administrative. Does the budget balance, is the marketing effective, can we make the online submissions process work? Stealing time to read through the manuscripts in a pile on the desk is the point at which we remember what all the admin support has been in aid of. Encountering 'Queen Tamp' or 'Owl', 'Dashboard' or 'August letter' for the first time and feeling them nudge the axis of our perspective for just a moment was a total privilege. Our thanks to Jane Commane and Kathryn Maris for the keen editorial judgement which brought these writers to our attention.

Congratulations to Geraldine, Maureen, Katie and Lucy – it's been our pleasure to work with Nine Arches and Kathryn to introduce their work to a wider audience. We've no doubt that this book will be the first of many with their names on the spines, and we will watch their bibliographies expand with pride. This volume is the start of a series of Nine Arches Press/ Poetry School collaborative publications. Poets everywhere – we hope you find pleasure, provocation and inspiration within its pages.

Julia Bird,
The Poetry School.

For further information about Primers and future opportunties as part of this pubishing and mentoring scheme organised by The Poetry School with Nine Arches Press, please see: **www.poetryschool.com**

Geraldine Clarkson

Geraldine Clarkson's poems have appeared widely in magazines, including in *The Poetry Review*, *The Rialto* and *Poetry*. She is a former Arvon / Jerwood mentee and winner of the Escalator Prize. In 2015, she won the *Poetry London* and *Ambit* competitions, as well as the Ver Poets Prize, the Magma Editors' Prize, and the Anne Born Prize. She was commended in the 2015 National Poetry Competition, and her first pamphlet is forthcoming from smith/doorstop in the Laureate's Choice series.

Publishers are sometimes inclined to reduce poets to a saleable blurb, as in 'This poet writes about [fill in autobiographical detail, misfortune or event]' but Geraldine Clarkson cannot be reduced: there is no straightforward 'about'. Clarkson converts unspecified grief, salvation and joy into exhilarating, whimsical music by way of her dynamic and transformative imagination. Her capacity to communicate abstract and fragmentary experience in an aurally thrilling manner is a rare gift. And while her poems take formal risks, they also suggest discipline and mastery, evoking a wide range of influences from Hopkins to Carson. Her poems invite and endure rereading, and her subject matter—elusive, dark and primal—produces in the reader a state of simultaneous discomfort and euphoria.

that light

they said I should go towards the light —
the last thing I wanted — that all-vacating
white, and I was a stone or two
overweight with tar and muck
I needed more time to work off
— a year, a month, if we're bargaining —
give me a hole, a wet gulley
to wait in, to rinse my tarry shoes
shrive me, and I will consult again
the gold-edged pages of my *Imitation*
the millionstarry oblivion
which made my 13-year-old heart
gallop into gloom — *renounce renounce* —
a startling bouncy break with pain
blandishments to let go and in one swoop
the pain stops, while voices far off
drown and I wave as happy
as a spider in lilied bullied twilight

        riddling light comes up to my ankles
        that's okay, you get used to icecapped toes
        damp arches, rheumy metatarsals
        and settle to make sense of dim bookless
        alleyways with their particular latrinalia —
        tearfelt messages in limestone and chert
        demanding headworm logic

and then a flock of patients in an antechamber
whom I am shocked to see need my help
and I am drafted in to put ticks in columns
of a log, to fetch gallons of spilling light

in buckets, fend off curdling flashes
of too black, too jagged, and have people laid
sleeping in my lap while I lift my head
and call out—my palms chafed from battling
cave crickets, sifting pebbles
sorting them in hollows as they gurgle
and suck themselves downstream
with an adult tang leaving me clear
my eyes sore with cataloguing, some dick
in charge bringing more record cards
and warmed laudanum

        I'm chanting psalms
       looking out for the light again
      around some sharp corner, exquisite
      and milk-bright to feed off, but
      not yet

Podcarp

She and three men-friends picnic at the edge of a podcarp forest: hot syrups and soda, blue cheeses, orange pickles, pink hams and oatmeal pancakes all set out on gingham. Paper napkins stick like dove-feathers to fingers as she turns to pore over a basket of photographs one of the m-fs has brought.

Sepia specials, seasoned and see-through, seeing through them into childhood rooms left ajar and chilled, seismically unaltered, the piano grinning and childless, the round table like a butterscotch pool, surrounded by plastic-topped stools, a world-weary stork beaten into their faces.

That room's function was grieving, knitted into the carpet, preserving its gold and blue swirls like miracles, *your one wild and precious life* pressed into it like underlay.

All generalisations are inane, especially this one. The three chaps were bored now and role-playing like a story of Bold, Squat, and Quaking. Bold and Squat just in from the country, Quaking wanting to go to Mass before the Ball. The forest too ancient to be real. Her poring spent, pores enlarged, Bold and Squat pawing the remains of the food, mucky rainclouds stealing west, loved ones loving and sleeping far away.

Of all the edible beds in this place, the one growing dandelions is the most healing. She lets her girl out at night to go gathering, as free and clear as a girl is, when not pressed on by a man or a mother. She drags things home in hessian, turns a burly sack on the windowsill to the watery dawn. Writes up notes and invigorates her enquiries with the sucking of chlorophyll into a fountain pen.

She asks for photos, photos, photos, and fills the basket, placing them in layers to weather. Blue matures to mildew-mauve and the forest prepares to sleep, chanting. Everyone loves and leaves except her.

'your one wild and precious life' is quoted from Mary Oliver's poem 'The Summer Day'.

Camelament

Whistle, *chica*,
whist. Give your ear
close and flutter. And flutter.
Eat in all you can hear.
Grow rotund on it, fit
as a fiddler's wife's
cat. There are other kinds
of right learning. Cause
you know. Cause you hear.
Bilge goes out with the suds.
A chain of Cheyennes
touches the lodge of
an enemy. You explode
flat on the floor. Fat
on fear. Flayed
with sharp and hot, and not.

Leaving Glawdom by night—

dressed glam in twisted serpent
bangles and a sly mothy stole
I set off north by north-east
for seven leagues until I met

the sea, arching Atlantic
coastline, white foam, high noise
and 3 youths, smiling, yelling
into the wind, selling

apples, peddling riddles.
I asked them how many years—
did they know— they called back
dozens; how far out to sea—

America; where the treasure
was— *in silver conches hanging*
from the wreck which pirates
ransacked last November.

I thanked them, pretending
to understand, and bought 3 russets,
rough and tawny, slid them
inside my knapsack and continued

south by south-west for thirteen
furlongs until I met
an old forest creaking
with gold and auburn baubles—

humming birds attending—
and squirrels swivelling rich trinkets
till the branches seemed to dance
and I thought I understood

and glanced around for maidens
I could quiz, but there were none
and I shrugged off my bag,
kicked loose my sandals, gripped moss

between my toes and smelled
woodsmoke, half-baked apples, saw
the whole darn forest
tonguing devilish

orange flames and I tried
to plot the hopping curlicue
edges with my pencil and my
compass and where were

those mystic maidens who could guide
and give me wisdom and suddenly
I heard them laughing, high-stepping
in a glade, they were rifling

plated conches full of treasure
dangling bracelets from their teeth
jewels banging on their chins
and I looked aghast—me a ghost

half-rubicund and silt with ash—
what could I ask?

Violette, Michaela et al, according to Mildred

What if it were all
an accident of alliteration
a serendipity of pinned-down sound?
[Letter from Mildred's penfriend, early September]

Violette
is cooled in a cocked hat, played to by viols in a lock-in at Ryans' Bar. She's a shivery walk on the strand at dawn with no sleeping, muck-tired, swaddled in a plaid blanket, a chieftain's sidekick. Film-makers set up a nostalgic scene at the beach graveyard, snaffling ideas from the real funeral on Tuesday. The same leather coat and Celtic cross. For the 'film funeral', the tide is a creased Galway shawl in the background and the double-bed grave of the couple who would not be parted is foreground. Brief blarting of 'Danny Boy'. She piles her hair up in October till they say she looks like a spring chicken. Lucky.

Michaela
is ten roubles for a gulag hotel, sharp and solitary as a *poustinia*. She speaks no words before noon, and till twilight only mumbles in lisping Spanish to her canary-lookalike parrot. He answers her in precise Old English and is critical. She dries her scrubbing brushes on the back step, leaves washing stretched over bushes in the clearing. Makes foot salve with fresh sage, for the days are long, and not long.

Valerie

is a collection of bird books, ragged at the edges, and marked with guano. She is especially volume 2, pages 69, Guillemot, and 70, Kittiwake. Her father is Kite, Birds of Prey, the returners, p 83, and her mother, Blackbird, British Favourites (p 100 and frontispiece). Her brother, Robin, is insouciant, head of the gang, with a brutish mating call.

Emily

is mapped onto shifting sand, her margins leaky and capricious. Each square of the grid deceptive, smoked. When the tide is out, the flats gleam like wet dog belly and look luscious to bury your nose into and inhale.

> *Postscript*
> I stopped askew and looked for you, blessings strewn like litmus paper after an alkaline experiment... Along the hunting halls, lewd trophies of gross-jowled reindeer, gorgons of sense, multi-layered ratcatchers of desire: Plantagenet surprise gives way to rued Tudor delight.
>
> *[Postcard from Mildred to her penfriend, late August]*

My Mother, the Monsoon

I go out early to do her messages, to avoid her brylcreemed exes who will dip in at the bookies, betting on snow for Christmas, rain on St Swithin's Day. And her brigade of lady-friends who breakfast, who finger meaty garnets at their throats and linger over each other's wrinkles, ogling. The comedy of correctness. Back home, the house is full of ticks; of mad cousins making money, breaking culture with karate chops, gnawing on it with their eyeteeth. Moderation is one over the top for the mother. Who is family for the old lady dwindling, circled by doctors and district nurses like the farmer's wife in her den? The beautiful and the stunned. I'm suddenly dumped into a whole year of mouldy Mondays, arcane and off the boil. Be still for the postman, lick his lovely thumb. Dumb-lovely, plump with packages. If you are good he will give you a neighbour's missive. It's not considered dishonest any more, he says, he has a dispensation and is probably double-jointed. This family is a becalmed army, idiot with sealed passion. Mother has climate change for a personality. I have become one of the draughts in a stately home, brocade-curtained and visited nostalgically. Don't take me for lost. I have cleaned the carpet of every room with my rasping tongue, rinsed each with tears. Don't take me for the host. Be sick, she says, it's less risky and you'd make a lovely corpse, chisel-cheeked, and modest. She rains for half my life.

Queen Tamp

The Queen has a glorious table, slicked and lunar, a floating lozenge, new-minted swimming pool, in her parlour. When she is out, we sneak books in there, dusty velvet-backed tomes hauled in from the library, mounds of them, breasting an orgy of knowledge—pert facts which beckon from the brimming disc. Warm volumes unlock homes in which the boy and girl inhabit brightly-lit rooms with pianos, butterscotch curtains, Sacred Hearts on flock-papered walls, a swell of laughter and a smell of everything being just right. If she comes back unexpectedly, we've learned the knack of sweeping the table's surface, getting everything out of sight, so that she finds us contemplating our reflections in smooth cherrywood, puffy red faces in the clear.

Some afternoons, on the rocks, the boy and I fish with makeshift lines. The water plays bear-backed in the sun or swirls like a pack of dogs in the wind. Often we've grasped something. I've held armfuls of fat thrashing pollock. When we've spotted her dear butlers approaching to look for us, the boy has made me dissimulate and sit on the silver liveliness – its delicate bulk has filled out, subtly amended with young.

When we awake

Four men at the bedside of a loved one. One moves forwards roughly – there is always one who has some thought, some shooting-up of emotion which he has bent back like steel, but whose springing forward into this curtained, candled closet of a room he cannot suppress (it is inevitable). A scuffle: voices raised and pulled down again, like foxes trying to escape over a fence. I speak a prayer and wake.

You are not here. Your footprints on the step would have been talisman against such terrors. I drift back. In the dream-room, the eldest brother – it is so obvious that they are brothers, the Slavic cheekbones, the gold-red hair – is livid, his face reflecting rays off the tucked-in body on the bed, whose carefully splayed limbs wait under the sheet, as if in anticipation of death-as-masseur. His eyes hook the younger brothers' eyes in a kind of hateful crochet. Murderous words like 'inheritance' hop in the static. The moon nudges in at the sash, open to gossip, eager to infiltrate moon-logic into this fetid man-hole. One brother snatches the curtain and secures it. I am praying again, involuntarily, the words tripping over each other like voyeurs pushing forward after an accident, the room rocking like a mad cradle.

Daylight. Curtains ripped open to reveal an icy but sun-hung morning, running with spring juices. In my room, fresh clutter – boots, a Bible, four men's jackets – relaxes into the general pile. Reek of candle-grease. My neck creaks, arms and legs need to be rubbed to life. I hear singing from below, a spindly strain circles the balcony. When we awake it will be like this.

Love Cow

Oh cow of love you have me pinned
to your evergreen felt

and are in at my ear with fermenting
oaths and actual importuning

and imprecations. I rebut you
with a tough raft of arguments, derived

from magazines under the sofa
at my Aunt Libbie's house

I have a disease, your rump is small,
your rich cream disgusts me

and others which are more
sophisticated, from the Bible and books of

philosophy. You give me a soft brown
stare. How I wobble now before you, cow

of love, humongous, like a free-range
sack of boulders swaying

delightfully, your cordial spine
rippling, your celtic skeleton

offering promise. To eat you
would be divine, surely,

your emerald milk fast-forwarding
to your stomachs, pressed over and over

by clenching muscles. Why is it you cows get
such bad press? I wonder, half-beguiled.

Sometimes I see you, fenced,
defending young ('let go of your dog

if cows surround you', the notice
on the farm gate says)

or at the abbatoir, steaming hot
and hung prosaically on hooks.

Or on the plate with no relief
except for some mocking green

salad— staked out, defenceless.
They say your flesh can stay

unsullied in the gut
for six months or more—

bowels fill with longing
for sloping fields, a faraway sea.

When tooraloos were taboo,

the old folks crouched in the hedges, soft peat leaking
between their toes, rubber bands curbing their fingers,
in a backspin as they tried to master the new rules.

Their tongues were trained in different shapes
from the ones the government was allowing now,
their throats once oiled with jugs of punch,

knees freighted with pretty wenches, one fine morning
in May... June, or July... by the Mountains of Mourne
or the Cliffs of Dooneen, wishing wishing wishing in vain

to be maids or youths again. Even whistles were
proscribed, and the joyful jig of the accordion
abandoned, which had set knees and heels

reeling and tapping. *She said come in, sir,
and meet my father...* Who knew when a tooraloo
would break loose and what it would do. In the end

you could always escape across the main, as many had before,
too-ra-loo-ra, to *Californ-eye-ay*, and instead of singing praties,
you'd be singing lumps of gold, too-ra-loo-ra-lay.

a young woman undressed me and

five minutes later she undressed me again
ten minutes after that she undressed me
and again fifteen minutes later
by which time I was beginning to feel tender
her fingers were cool and her palms firm
as she disembarrassed me of one hot layer
after another: tweed, cotton, nylon, loosing
buttons and cuffs, unravelling ties

when she had been undressing me for a month
I dared to say, sideways, my mouth under the chest
of a pullover which she was easing over my head
with such skill and love that my adams apple
felt like it had been rolled in honey
and rubbed in oats, and my voice was grungy
and low, my skin somewhat shiny
and raw: *muhuuhu muhuuhu ph ph ph hmmhu hm*
she touched my lip with a shapely thumb
shhh, don't fret. her voice like jinxed june breezes
in lime leaves. and then. her voice like rills rushing over flint
and dazzling in sunlight. we'll get you undressed and then
we'll see to that. just a moment now. and still
she continues to undress me

Declare

In the *clair* of the morning, a streaky-bacon sky, unkosher dawn, me tumbling to prayer, still at the unclean edges of it, my morning self dipped below the surface, just starting to steep, the first psalm half-unravelled, when

the wedge of the attic fills full-tilt with an impatient important egg-yolk wash, water sucked through a plug, backwards. And two-thirds of the way into the room, at the golden section, an ivory figure with forearms extended, bristling

with razor-rays and a curious asking asking. Two ivory fists in front of my face – 'right or left?' he quizzes me, me wordless fool of a girl opening opening. He flips a fist to reveal a golden sliver, a lip, a pip he plants in me

like pre-flesh, a shiver of ice to steal my breath, bind up my yesses and noes. A seed word, syllable, choking over and over, promising to tell tight salt things I want to shut my ears to. Then me hotfoot to Elizabeth, skimming

rough hillsides like a ducks-and-drakes pebble, the syllable guttering over and over, me trying to outpace it. And then E! rubicund, humble puffed-out and plumped wineskin, replete. And the pip shaking me

to bless her, to sport with her child, the two of us mothers circled in a hoary girdle, like a cat's cradle, blushing at each other, our bellies brought into contact, kissing, me sensing the rough spurt of the one who is before the one he is to go before.

Maureen Cullen

Maureen Cullen wrote poetry as a teenager, returning to it after a career in social work, inspired by her Open University tutor. She has since obtained a Masters in Creative Writing from Lancaster University, where she studied poetry and short stories.

Maureen Cullen's poetry has an intense, immediate power. The irresistible pull of the voice that inhabits each of these poems is clear, insistent; it is a tug not just on all the right emotional keys, but one which evokes the rich, physical sounds and shapes of language and memory. Her use of dialect is precise, crafted with a keen ear to fine-tune the vigorous and tender music of her poetry. This results in poems taut with a perfect tension, beautifully and sparely constructed, and acutely direct. The achievement of Cullen's poems is not just their intense musicality and observation, but their ability to catch a child's voice 'just so', and to grow confidently into that voice as the protagonist, Maisie, grows into adulthood. Throughout, Cullen allows her language to sing, rich and candid, on themes of searching and belonging, family and coming-of-age.

Note: As part of what is intended as a wider collection, these poems are a chronological sequence, snapshots of points in Maisie's life as she moves through foster care as a young child, to adoption and finally as a young adult to contemplating her birth family. Adult Maisie begins from 'Scots Rose'.

A Case o Fraud

Ma foster mammy, Val
gied me a photae wi ma egg roll
tae pit on the wall at nursery

o ma foster sister
as a teeny baby
wi her baw cheeks an snottery nose.

Ah didnae tell

when teacher said ah wis pretty
an pressed it wi her thumb
tae the middle o the sunny daffodil.

Annalise's Stars

No tae suck yer thumb at school
No tae wet yer knickers
No tae shout an no tae squeal
No tae cheek yer betters

    If yer guid she gies ye stars
    an if yer bad – she disnae

No tae pick yer nose an chew
No tae flick yer fingers
No tae spit oot lumpy stew
No tae play wi scissors

    If yer guid ye pick yer stars
    an if yer bad – ye cannae

No tae steal the baby's rusk
No tae scuff yer trainers
No tae elba in an push
No tae go wi strangers

    If yer guid ye'll be her star
    an if yer bad. Jist say sorry

Revolving Door

At Kelvingrove Art Gallery and Museum

Jump in quick,
shoes pressed thegither,
shove the gold rail
till it gies a groan.

Too soft,
it scissor-sticks,
forgets tae spill ye oot
the ither side,
trapped in the windae,
grown-ups cannae hear ye.

Shove too hard,
ye cause a stir,
burl forever
in foster circles,
yer too much
trouble Maisie,
aw the gawpin faces
meltin
intae wan great oooohhh…

When it rumbles tae a stop
aw they find's
a button, some crayons,
a jotter o bird families
an a half-sooked
sherbet lolly.

New Shoes

Ah sat tae lunchtime wi ma new shoes on,
suitcase packed tae bustin in the hall.
Annalise wis mutterin on the phone
wi the social worker, Jim, aboot the papers.
Whit tae sign, why wis she left hersel
tae sort this oot the day? New parents due
in five minutes an Maisie bleached as a sheet,
up in the toilet half the night. Ah tellt
her ah'd be good. She jist wiped ma snot away.

Ah sat tae teatime wi ma new shoes on,
suitcase unpacked, empty in ma room.
The social worker, Ann, wis mutterin
wi ma new parents, whit tae sign, how best
tae help me settle in. The house smelt
o daffodils an Dettol. An books.
An ah couldnae flush the pan. Ah said,
please can ah go home? Ann didnae hear,
jist smiled, unclasped finger efter finger.

On Two Wheels

Come on, Daddy Eddie said
and bounced the frame –

looped one arm under ma oxter
lurched me up tae the saddle –

jist two wheels tae take
the bend o the brae. Whit if

ah got sliced by the ice cream van
or bevelled intae the postbox –

ah gripped the handlebars
flexed ma soles on the pedals –

one wobble, off thegither –
his hand a hoverfly at ma back.

Owl

Teacher gied us an exercise
tae draw a picture of our *fathers*.

I drew an owl, coloured it in
wi shades of plaid, gied it glasses

like pennies. Owls wear glasses, I said,
cause they're smart. I drew him a tie

like he wore for the church, a cap
for his clump of ginger feathers, sat

him on a branch of our oak tree
wi his Golden Virginia, a red spot

on the doup at his lip, smoke puffing
tae the top of the page, wished he'd fly,

stretching wing-tip tae wing-tip
but maybe he'd cough, need his back clapped.

I leant his walking stick on the bark
so he could wing-limp up the path.

Apprentice

Talc patted tae a peely-wally tinge,
I stuck out my tongue for her tonsil test.
She hummed and hawed,
said I wisnae well at aw,
squirrelled doon tae Spar
for Aspirin, Tunes, my weekly Bunty.

She made her special chicken broth.
I didnae dare tae lick the bowl.
Nettled wi lies I napped.

Bucked up at four,
the bell ringing school out
ower the mill dam. Bored,
I snaked ontae the kitchen stool,
mouth soon thick wi cinnamon.

My nails traced sugar diamantés
as she wheeled the china plate
through the crook of her hand, right thumb
scalloping the tacky trim,
at her elbow a messed up mound
of mottled skins. I set three leaves
clover neat, a promise
tae crisp on teeth at suppertime.

Flour kissed, she bent tae the apples
snug in the oven,
unwrapped her apron,
swirled me another pill.

Peely-wally: pale, sickly

Wee Wifie

Puddle milk on her worktop
she'll curdle it wi an eyebrow.

Leave trainers in a heap
pick your way ower hot tracts.

Answer her back
dinnae hang about.

But when the headmaster
said my *impertinence*

was in the genes
she minced his tongue

wi her high speed
rotary mammaries.

Scots Rose

On Friday, I visit the Royal Infirmary
tae find Dad nestled in the green
of the Necropolis. Who thocht
it was therapeutic
tae put dyin auld men in trolleys
set tae the tilt of gravestones?

I cradle his purpled hand.

Saturday, I'm in the garden
where you'd never guess
tae look at the gnarled stems,
that past the brush and bruise,
the rot, the liverish leaf,
is a single rose.

It stuns the hedge pink.

Dreaming Mum

She began tae speak, tae move about her flat,
washing up at the scratched metal sink
wi her seventh floor, eagle-eye view
of a hotchpotch of roofs. Easterhouse
or the Gorbals. Might be Drumchapel.

Tight and wiry in her vinyl pinny,
she mops the linoleum, squelches
the head dry. I watch her from the door
and when she turns, she smiles wi teeth
that dinnae quite fit. She has my mole
on her right cheek, my golf ball breasts.

She boils the kettle, brews tea
in her tannin-lined pot, lifts out mugs
wi sunflowers on. We munch caramel wafers.
Between chews, she says, *my beautiful girl,*
comes so near I can hear her breath,
see the craters of her tongue
as she dabs crumbs from the corner
of my mouth, our eyes half-closed.

Milk Tooth

Swaddled in paper
tucked intae a thimble
a tussle of tissue
flowers in my palm.

I peel apart the petals
peer at a moon chip
the fractured tepal
of a white china lily
a fragment of bone.

Out of cavity it wobbles
threads back intae gum
latches tae areola
takes the kick of colostrum
sucks and swallows.

The Sisters

After a Painting by Mary Cassatt

After their nap, they sit thegither
in their white Sunday dresses,
identical in sisterhood, a year
or two between them, differences
blurred by the living-green
of brush-stroked grass. One hangs
on the other's neck, hand loose
at the orbit of her cheek – the tilt
of their heads, bone tae bone.

Four chestnut eyes fixed ahead,
no knowing when the artist
gathers up her oils and brushes,
the frocks are hung in the armoire
and they must go their separate ways.

Strangers

At the first floor landing
the moon's bawface
spills milk ower the close.

A guy bowls by, tarring
my mouth wi smoke.
His 'Ye awright, hen?' tumbles

tae the street. At home
in the shoebox,
the Polaroid photo.

I bring him up, oil-black
in overalls,
fag ash spotting his palm.

My skin chafes on rough
as he bumps me,
a fitbaw on his knee.

The Thin Place

I climb up the scree tae the spot
where you smile in the photo,

unaware I'm already
a speck in your belly.

Behind us, the bridge sits at the shoulder
of the auld house, blind witness

tae the plunge of the ravine
where the burn slip-slides below.

Here the faerie world quicksteps
intae our own, a Thin Place

where we're free tae meet again.
The clock ticks backwards, a gift

tae best friends at the balustrade
in our white cotton frocks,

auburn sifting sunlight,
dandelion seeds at our lashes.

A Thin Place in Scots mythology is a permeable
boundary between the spirit world and Earth.

Saumon

I take the Caledonia bus
tae my mother's town,
skip off at the bridge,
pat the note in my pocket,
a scrawled address.

Fingers stretched
tae the teasing foam,
I'm mesmerised
by shoals of saumon
swarming up-river.

They belly-slap
slabber stones,
whip wellie boots,
slip the heron's harpoon,
intent on nothing

but memories
of their homing grounds,
the scent of tail,
fin, scale,
the sweel of birth.

I loose my scrap of paper
intae the broil
and clap my ears
against the heckle
of sacrificial waves.

The Gloamin

The bulk of him at the back of our yard,
shirtsleeves rolled tae the anvil
of each elbow, working a spade.

I wait at the kitchen door, neither in nor out,
hand on the jamb, mouth thick
wi peat and wrenched grass.

Night gathers him up an inch at a time
as he digs out potato trenches, dirt flitting
in clumps, bed sheets trembling like ghosts.

I will him tae turn, tae swagger
down the path, dark in denim,
the steel of the barrow scything black.

Ready tae conjure up the planes of his face,
I bind my breath tae the crunch of gravel,
the thud of his spade set against our wall.

Katie Griffiths

Katie Griffiths grew up in Ottawa, Canada – the daughter of Northern Irish parents. She returned to the UK for university and subsequently worked at *Radio Times*, then as volunteer co-ordinator for refugees of the war in the former Yugoslavia, and as teacher at a further education college. Her collection *My Shrink is Pregnant* was joint runner-up in the 2014 Poetry School/Pighog Poetry Pamphlet Competition. She is singer-songwriter in the band A Woman in Goggles, under which name she also blogs.

In Katie Griffiths' steely and unsettling poems, there's a deft journalistic approach, yet her writing does so much more than simply 'report back' on experiences, people and places encountered. This is an alert and nimble kind of poetry, and Griffiths possesses a dexterity which allows her poems to shift into a variety of voices and yet still firmly occupy her own, to move through landscapes and know exactly which details and images will stick with us the longest and matter the most. Often, she focuses in on the strangeness of absences – the vanished bridges and minarets of the post-war Balkans, a solar eclipse, or language's naming of our losses. Her poems don't dodge the gaps but rather approach them at distinctive and off-kilter angles, finding an alternative lens through which to focus her wry perspectives; often astonishing, sometimes grimly vivid, always unexpected.

Capo

The farmyard rule of who's boss: my chicken-strangling hands getting instant results, squeezing the upper register out of a neck, forcing it to shriek falsetto, cutting airflow and blood supply just this side of suffocation, just enough to allow what's wedged under my armpit to flap wings, like that song I tried to strum when we sat on your bed in your host's house the summer I turned seventeen, on school exchange in Wilhelmshaven, and you handed me a worn guitar I couldn't subdue without the throttlehold, the tourniquet of a capo clamped to its fifth fret. The instrument struggled, whimpered like a mandolin, my voice wavered, fingers slid on strings, your legs too skinny, too close. You tried to kiss me before we left. No sooner outside the front door, your host-mother banged open the shutters of your room above us, shot out her head, a clock's crazed cuckoo jumping the hour, that scrawny bald neck, ligaments straining, its pronouncement shrilling down the street: *Du hast mit ihm im Bett geschlafen.*
*Du dreckiges Mädchen, dreckiges Mädchen.**

*You slept with him in bed. You dirty girl, dirty girl.

The Friends You Keep

Zagreb's dark backstreets spat you out
with your upturned collar, slicked hair
and height that forces me to angle my face
into the sting of sleet. I can't place you –
not charity or aid worker, but a fixer of sorts,
my escort towards the bus stop along a row
of lime trees gagged in December ice.
We board the 201, you clutch my elbow
like a tiller, steer me to the one vacant seat,
hold dominion over the stuffy interior
with an English voice unreeling names
recognised by sullen passengers:
Karlovac, Franjo Tuđman, the Krijena.
Then you change tack, cite clips from your life,
the shooting weekends, dumped fiancée,
boarding-school pranks, how you clicked apart
the shoulder sockets of the mute boy
until he bleated that his name was *Gordon.*

I breathe mustiness from your sodden overcoat.
You ask why I'm in this place, nice girl like me.
I shrug: *the arguments, the bickering.*
You claim you can arrange an end to all that,
easy as a nod,
as an envelope of (preferably) Deutschmarks,
as a phone call to those friends you keep.

The Road to Split

This could not be England,
this stand-off of land and water
and the road that forms the seam between.
Nor these signs that man
has scrabbled to put order into rocks,
small clawings of territory,
minute fields dragged from the granite.

Past abandoned habitations
and the barefaced chill of Pag Island,
we creep across a pontoon understudy
of the Maslenica Bridge, shelled to hell,
photographing neither gun emplacements
nor the way winter has cast
its snow in slapdash swirls.

The chain-smoking bus driver
pumps radio oompah through the coach,
swamps the soundtrack of *Top Gun* – no protest
since all eyes are stuck to Croat subtitles.
In deep ravines at every savage bend vehicles rust:
perhaps dumped for convenience, or perhaps
the road, pulled too far south, has flexed its spine.

The Knight of Swords

Matthew, hammered by sun, sprawls
on the spare bed in my room. Antiseptic
cream makes him a B-movie ghoul.
Hiatus. Whiff of strawberry perfume
across my wrists. Everyone has dispersed,
the devoted to trail a Medjugorje priest,
the motivated with tapes to size up damage,
the boy adventurers to Mostar to grab action
with HVO before dinner, though to avoid
our awkward questions they keep
their army fatigues in the next village.

As news photographer, Matthew's paid
to snap close shaves, yet can't compete
with the lens of the sniper from Toulouse.
Jenny enters, pockets bulging with a pack
of cigarettes, pack of Tarot. In moments
of crisis it's even stevens which one she'll
reach for, but jeez it's so hot, we'll run with
anything: sorcery, premonition, the Chariot,
the Tower, the Knight of Swords on his white
charger, weapon upraised - who knocks at
our door, minutes later, back in his civvies.

HVO – the Croatian Defence Council, involved in
operations in and around the Mostar area

A Lack of Minarets

From a distance something is wrong,
a skyline tampered with, hard-edited.
As the bus coils down the mountainside
into the basin of Mostar,
a dampening of voices gives time
to ponder that what's awry
is the city's heart,
charred, glassless and emptied out.

This is the home of the dispossessed,
shunted like marbles from zone
to zone, who pick their way
past commandeered cars
and makeshift kiosks sprouting
at odd corners to replace
shops that once packed the town.
Spring sidles in tentative, unremarked.

Inside my borrowed flat I trip
on the owners' void, their pictures
and mementoes a deadweight.
Impossible to see through grubby
UNHCR plastic, stretched
to soften the windows' absence,
whether Serbs lie in wait
up on Mount Hum, lost in snow.

Past curfew, with the moon
a weak salve on dark buildings,
their amputations, their spilling stones,
I walk the former front line
to a rowdy cavern restaurant,
where glasses clink toward the photo
of the now-dead owner diving
close by, off the ancient Stari Most.

I step outside. The old bridge
has been blown to pieces, I know –
in blackness the Neretva snags
on rubble heaped in its way.
But the night is sly, for I'd swear
the arch is still high above me,
a cupped hand about to swipe,
and all the air teetering.

Dashboard

And this Leonard who maintains
his convoy discipline, steady speed,
never tailing the bumper in front;

and this Leonard whose wife
has draped half the lorry cab in rosaries,
china Madonnas, and shampoo bottles

filled with holy water, as if Catholicism
has set up camp and is evangelising
through postcards of pilgrimages past;

and this Leonard whose portion
of the dashboard has seen the sacking
of the monasteries, or perhaps a purge

by Presbyterians, with every statue siphoned
and idolatry swept aside, *no Pope here,*
all his driving space pristine;

and this Leonard, leather patches
on his sleeves, who heaves aid boxes
in the warehouse with its corrugated roof

where curious villagers gather to check
what the British trucks have in store
and soldiers direct items to special corners;

and this Leonard, shocked at the square meal
in the scrubbed dining room of the *pension*
when 'surely this town is under siege',

who swigs a glass of slivovitz in the local bar
(with the man who drove out in a plumbing van)
while his wife nips to the church for mass;

and this Leonard who today
in the foyer is propped by two people
as if he is a monument about to fall

because he has just seen the Virgin,
her blue robe billowing, fiery halo
scorching her head, light sizzling

from her feet, hands folded in prayer,
as she hovered by his bed
while he took an afternoon nap;

is this exact same Leonard, whose wife weeps
joyous tears and will buy perfect souvenirs,
enough to see the whole dashboard filled.

The Urbane Terrorist

His checklist of venues: Gaza, Grozny, Mostar,
is tucked in his uniform, carefully packed.
A match tossed here, few bullets sprayed there,
he excels in the short recreational contract.

He uses semtex and riddles, rope-wire and jokes,
an array of devices, whatever's at hand,
to infiltrate, flummox, ingratiate, coax,
he's a master at sniffing the lie of the land.

Back home, Oxbridge circles think he's hot news,
savour his chutzpah, and how he rejects
tired notions of Tolstoy, Kerouac, Ted Hughes:
ideas shown off like a muscle being flexed.

He cuts out the dross, sloughs off admirers
who stack like reminders unanswered for days.
His eyes are quarrels that sizzle, catch fire,
nothing's unsinged in the path of his gaze.

For if noticed by him, it's a white-knuckle ride
into new waters, your old life adrift.
You'd be joining the ranks of those who confide
that, on his say-so, they'd leap off a cliff,

like the convent girl, who beneath him now lies,
this slow, cool, mothering Sunday, undressed,
discovering how itchy are the hairs of his thighs,
how loud the skirmishes inside his chest.

Leaving

This is how a nation cold-shoulders you.
It herds you into an airport concourse,
feeds you from cartons laid out on the floor,
labels you as *refugee* on express to the front,
though a clutch of relatives harrows your passage.
On the plane, your child will cry.
A hilarious Englishman will shout: *give that baby a gin.*

Skew this slightly, this setting sail.
It could be famine,
or the simple outgrowing of shoes.
It could be dusk, a foghorn throating,
lights juddering on Liverpool docks,
and your mother's eyes
drenched with three thousand miles of ocean.

A Haircut for Radovan Karadžić
Before the International War Crimes Tribunal

When it comes to style, I cannot decide,
steady my scissors behind this neck
where hairs thicken to a wayward mane

tinged brute metallic. Of colourings
I know something: that glimpse of two
white-headed children from Vukovar

on the bus. I'd never thought how terror
can seed, grow its flora through a scalp.
Later in a fuggy gymnasium,

home to three hundred hauled as freight,
(four days without food or water)
I met young Kemal, his hair confettied

with white eggs of lice. He greeted me
by kicking my shins, though mine
was the last sighting across barbed wire

of his older brother, coiffed at Manjača,
eyes to the ground, shorn by smirking captors.
I saw how the sudden sentence of baldness,

how the head in its new nakedness
did not subtract but précised him
to a distinctive line drawing.

Cutting implements heat my hand.
My client waits, hair barging his collar.
When it comes to style, I cannot decide.

A Village Priest and I Watch the Solar Eclipse Through the Safety of a Kitchen Colander

Our backs to the window, I sieve daylight
       across a piece of paper. Tricked by the pattern

of a hundred tiny suns, he is unaware that rules
       will soon be broken, has never seen a child

interrupt a sprinkler or a catamaran swerve
       in front of a ferry, flouting shipping lanes.

That the moon should be so dissident –
       make a beeline into another's orbit and hog the limelight –

is an effrontery he wants to ignore. But the sun winces.
       The sky behind us falters.

The bright circles on the page are overcome. I give him
       the colander to hold. He scoops his hand inside

as though it is a tadpole net whose dark wriggling catch
       must, like salt, be thrown over his shoulder.

Tips for a Post-War Correspondent

Locate an unoccupied café table,
your face towards the harbour
where Jadrolinija ferries glide to Brač.
Open your notebook.

A target approaches, that young man
mantled in old man's frame.
He finds you, asks:
You eat lungs?

Don't lose focus, though he has,
with his flourish of postcards
all stamped and addressed to you.
Agree with him that, yes,

it is you in the creased photos
he now also waves under your nose.
You. His long-lost, long-limbed *Nicolette*,
though you never lazed in unmown grass.

Admire the battered tin star he's pinned
to a dog-eared certificate in child's
boisterous script that names him
Nicolaj, and sheriff of this town.

He's come to reclaim you
after his twelve years in secure wards,
first inland, at Bihać, then institutions
creeping ever closer to the sea.

You eat lungs?
He gulps an oblong capsule,
one of two a day that keep him steady.
His chest rises and falls like tide-turn.

If you flinch you'll miss the stumble
of Croat consonants across his tongue.
Lunch. He means *lunch*.
Do you want to eat *lunch*?

Simple. He is Nicolaj.
You can play Nicolette,
not just here for the pickings and spoils,
your legs lengthening towards his chair.

Soil

Take measure of my depths. Use a flagpole
that impales. Scrabble with your naked hands.
       I'm full of fingernails.

You'll hear my grains are rowdy like war drums
in their hurry, sending boots to march across me.
       Men fall. I drink their fury.

Yet in peacetime I'm engorged with scattered tin
and bone, the centuries of keepsakes
       you cherish or disown.

To remind you of this footing, I'll fasten
to your shoes, function as an anchor
       you'd be wise not to lose

until the ground-rules shift on that morning
when you die. Then I'll overturn the system,
       be completion, be your sky.

I Waved my Placard

The words on my placard were unplanned but fierce.
They said: *The universe empties itself at night*
although I'd run out of space and *at night*
had to be scrawled on the back. I must confess
I'd cribbed the thought, maybe from a billboard,
maybe from a flyer, maybe from tickertape
in the technology museum, where every exhibit
from those computer teething years was laughably
innocent. Yet I waved my placard as if I'd kicked
butt with *ban the bomb*, then Greenham Common,
then the G8 summits – troughs more like – now
anti-austerity, rampant greenhouse gas, and Greece
putting the wind up the euro.

I waved my placard like dictum, like knell. I waved
until it and I were a metronome ticking through
the 10 o'clock news, until the stick in my hand
protested its wood beginnings and grew leaves
like spear thrusts, until its handle reverted to trunk
with the faces of my trapped ancestors begging to be carved,
until my fingers could no longer circle a whole tree
propelling me to a place with no ceiling.

Words for Sorrow

When my great-grandmother
discovered she was the last speaker
of the mid-west dialect,
she ditched her songs
of wind and tumbleweed
to mime for me
ten words for sorrow.

Her garments were eased
to show a sorrow that salted
deep folds in her skin.
That rose and hooked
the back of her throat.
That contoured
into an hourglass,

squeezing the very rasp
out of her. And how
the same word, with new
inflection, connoted a type
that flowed swiftly
and formed a gully
she could not wade.

She taught me
the word for sorrow
that out-shrieks darkness.
That descends like gauze,
yet no beast can rip through.
A kind that fastens itself
to the span of just one day

or to a jutting peg
where cast-off jackets droop.
And when her hands
measured empty space, I saw
it made a difference whether sorrow
remained the vehicle,
or became the entire road.

Lucy Ingrams

Lucy Ingrams has had poems published in various magazines, including *Poetry Ireland Review, Ink, Sweat and Tears, Agenda* and *Magma*. In 2015, she won the Manchester Poetry Prize, and in 2016 she won the *Magma* poetry competition. She is currently studying on the MPhil Creative Writing programme at the University of South Wales. She lives in Oxford.

Lucy Ingrams possesses a highly confident ear. Her syntax has an almost reckless exuberance, she leaps easily from one form to another, and her lines achieve an intense, breathy syncopation. Her musical skills, along with a broad palette of vocabulary that includes idiosyncratic kenning-like compound words, suggest she has borrowed techniques and attributes from Alice Oswald, Ted Hughes and other inheritors of the Anglo-Saxon tradition. And while her poems, like theirs, are interested in the natural world, she is ultimately more invested in human experience: she communicates love, anxiety and joy in original and thrilling poems.

Signs

And whether you loved me   loved me not
would come with a letter   come with you
would come   would come with some sign
of which there was no sign   yet

and yet   when it came   a letter (not you)
scribbled with signs   coding your answer
I put it by on the table   walked out into fields
hung with signs of their own   of spring breaking

through   wearing them naked as gooseflesh
still   and looked for a text to hook yours to
red in the willow crowns   plum in the birch
patterns of gnats   looked for a language

larger than us   *tremor of catkins*
folds of a bud   for meanings like runes
harder than answers   *length in the light*
the over and over of wood pigeon music

am out here still   waiting still longer   sure only
I'm not   whether you love me   love me not
flowering stars on the blackthorn bars   and at dusk
Sirius setting   Leo rising   or neither   and both –

June

You watch the sea from the doorway, while I look up grasses.
The wind showed me them: I'd gone out searching for bright breaths
of flower and come back tuned to fine-jointed staves,
shy-coloured panicles. My grass book (which thrives
on the dry) tells me in millimetres of common
couch culms – when you tell me we've lost the horizon.
We stare out, mourning dimension … flat as the waves'
skin, the sky's hang, now a low fleece
of fog wraps the chord-line between them,

         until
I try this: tail you to the fields, lie us down, show you the frail
fastenings, like hair, weaving Earth to the air, turn
us over, find out small hollows among the stems – a lichen
scrape, a whisking feather, a skylark's gaze, hummocks of heather –
and slowly, our seeing cups again, regains curvature.

A hearting space
– the hollow between two skins of wall. *Dry Stone Walling Terms*

Elsewhere we are as sitting in a place where sunlight
Filters down, a little at a time.   *John Ashbery*

He couldn't tell what his feelings were then: had formed instead a cairn-making habit – small markers along the way raised from skirmishes between his lived experience and his thought – hoping that one might open soon: a door on to his unseen.

Walking in winter fields one afternoon, he'd watched his dog plant its hind legs wide and tensile, as three deer bounced away from it – their pied, plié-ing rumps synchronising in anticipation of the chase – and it struck him, at once, that the trouble with story

is that it has too much gradient, is for ever tipping up or down hill, like those deer, turning everything between into so much traction. *How to un-truck from it?* he'd asked himself, as he spoke to his dog severely.

Later, she'd shown him a flock of waxwings flitch their way round a berry-tree, ruthlessly light as they cropped it – and been drawn only to a blackbird planted heavily nearby, witness to the attenuating dusk.

Hey, hey? she'd asked,

so he'd explained about the tipping deer, and how he wondered if the blackbird, unlike the dog, had un-coupled itself from story? How, come to think of it, he'd felt attracted for weeks now to the floors of valleys, level bodies of water, flat roofs, table mountains—

Next morning, he'd been tempted to call her in much the same vein: *Just here, on the patio flags, where the neighbour's cat lies taking the January sun … just here, something might show itself, a point of origin open…*

But when the cat lifted its bedazzled head, he'd thought he read in the prick of its ears that this was no more than yearning on his part, and planted the phone back in its holster. (Whereupon it rang – and was someone else entirely.)

Whether from doubt, or the nature of the exercise, these cairns of his always stayed blind, though stray cracks of light shone on his increasing skill at placing dry stones. Even so, he resolved to keep building them – doggedness being close to, if not actually, a feeling.

So will there be apples?

Cold nights   clear days   the fruit trees'
soft raised spurs   all thought of
him rinsed with light: *promise me —*
and then?   the hedges whisper in
new viridian dialects   willow-wrecks
leaf into bird-houses   and
          she is distracted,

keeps coming up against singulars: a
bicycling girl, her basket plaited
with hawthorn   *when will it rain?*
  – it will *rain*   a blackbird's
tv-aerial aria   this blue match
to a log – flame licking
          the emerald evenings.

and now he is lost to her   if she looks for him
in the greenwood will she find herself
lose herself?   'frost in May'   her friends
are afraid for her   at what stage
of a fire is the term 'conflagration'
applied?   *so many promises*
          she goes out   she goes looking ...

how can anyone stand this much
tenderness,   the woods holding the last
of the day in their arms?   she wishes
a hawthorn bicycle, a path home   instead a
quiet fine rain begins: *your promise*
– kept,   so if I find you   will there be apples,
          where now there are sleeves of blossom?

what if there's no further trace of him
    before nightfall?   the bird-houses
trip with alarm calls   her every step
        carefully —

August letter

In the dream you were – how were you? – whole, humorous, young. I must write and tell you. Your skin shone.

I must write and tell you that I dreamt of you last night. And other news – one friend makes her will, another plans his wedding for the spring.

It seems a time of year when people turn, address themselves. The moulting birds, too, empty the sky. Instead, colours move now on the wings of butterflies – arguses and tortoiseshells cherish the eyes of asters over and over.

I want to tell you how the year to me from August appears upside-down, like a tumbler tipped out. I peer into its tunc, and trace a tiny counterpoint: snow hyacinths on a tablecloth, winter coats on chairs pushed back, the smell of pears.

And I must ask you if you saw it too – perhaps our gazes met on its third eye – last week's low-rise blue moon? In my dream, your look ran clear, ran green.

The evenings here are long still, are they with you? Yet I find I plant mine up with candlelight, burn apple-wood – watch the mirror catch and flush.

This month's like that, a flare I want to boost. That even so will carry summer out upon its bier. My fingers flutter like the leaves to think of it.

In the dream, your hands were empty – full of your touch. If you were here, I could put mine out and you could take them.

Slow air
on a theme by Robert Burns

my
  heart   my
    heart's   my

in the moor-
  land   the mainland   the low-
    lands   the islands   the high—

my heart   my
  heart's not   my heart
    isn't

is chasing   is chaste for   is
  wandering   is wan
    for   wonders after

its dear,   and where-
  ever I   ever I
    go   go now,

my dear,   not to havens   to
  lochans   not to
    forests   to firths

my
  heart   my
    heart's   my

is near you   's never
  far from   isn't
    here

Stonechat's song

From a dock top, rain
on the still sand, rain
on the sea that's not, through
every nest of every
fulmar on the rocks —

       Flit to tell you

from a thistlehead, wind
kneading the loch, witching
for thirty from an alder's
sixty degrees, scything
midge ceilidhs —

       Flit to tell you

from a whin mast, flower
holes in the heather, kingcups
through the horsetails, eyebright
on the paths —

       Flit to tell you

from a marram pin, clouds
slow as junks, bagging
then loosing the light —
cloud washing,
a skyful —

       Flit to show you

the moor in sections,
rain wind flower cloud —
chit-chit-chit stone-chatterer,
though stones themselves
lie close and quiet, like love.

Leaf litter

I thought I would descend
into remembering love   so   *Grace Paley*

I was remembering love as I set out on an October walk
among trees. (You may think I must mean by that 'among
woods', but the place I was in was open and I followed paths
an unknown mower had mapped ahead of me.)

The smell of rain, the char of blown blackberries and pleats
of honey fungus all intensified my mood. Soon, every tree
I stopped at had the air of a past sweetheart. A yellow
tug of birch leaves rushed me back to Ray Doyle's hair on
Summer hill.

Light and space around each tree, like hindsight, sharpened
me. It was uncanny how I saw the dying fall inside a belling
spread, want within a crop of mast or berries, wellness in
burrs and galls among the branches. (Finally.)

Reaching a change, where one oak stood close enough
beside a beech to weave a shadow, I looked a long time
at the leaves they'd shed between them. It truly was some
mulch; you should have seen it … intricate, like aisle
mosaic to a cathedral altar … vivid as a *dhurrie* knotted

in the Sindh. No question, such a blanket could impede the
course of ice – do more: send up sparks, in time, ethereal
as bluebells, sharp as ramsons, whips already lit on paths
not open for me to see.

And by this staring into darkness, this savouring of decay, I
recollected (or collected?) what you're sure to keep in mind:
the autonomy of love, its self-sufficiency. Underground, or
over winter, love banks up – but will flare out again.

Snow tide

Between them, snow
and the light have scissored
a high new world of silver
woods and stiffened pools
that jackdaws tack unsteadily.

*

Winter chafes us orderly:
we open paper doors to advent days,
stand on the step for the solstice moon,
measure the shrink of mercury.

*

She starts, '*You are my … my…?*'
We laugh and answer, '*… daughters!*'
It takes no hold, she starts
again, stirs salt into our tea.

*

I trace the valley's freeze. Only
the gas-holder breathes – rises
or sinks in its lung-rings
to a rhythm that doesn't seize.

*

The thaw steals in,
like perfidy. Snows leak
down to jetsam heaps.
Barns, pylons, trees
stagger at the low horizons –

as grief might strand a woman, say,
feeling her mind's flood recede.

In the half-light,

we stop to study the moor's winter shawl
– tissue-crisp heather, leached moss, old grass straws –

when a rag of it sails loose, skims a camber of hill
(floating not on the wind but its will),

settles back to where it settled before
and knows something is new:

its wild sensor face, like a radio dish,
yaws two hundred and twenty degrees,

milling the twilight, listening for voles,
then, hearing the feed of our watching-it too,

statues.   And now
eons of eerie   unfold,

every pinprick of moor
webbed in a spell,

which we finally
        break,

boots flinching home
through the reach of its night-gaze.   Still

it stays still, moccasin-soft on its perch place,
head-to-tail curved like a rind of new moon.

Pinkfoots

We are just settling to the monotony of the drive, I think,
when you swing right, and the car fills up
with the spit and crack of rubber over open track.

A few more yards and we're cresting the low hills
that ring Meikle loch. You brake, snuff the engine, the lights –
and we are all ear, in the new dark, changing worlds.

In the wake of the car's throb, an eerie hubbub boils:
we are not alone, you guessed the geese might be here.
The hills bob with dim question-mark heads.

I push my door open. Thatch of February fields
and the sweet and metal of loch water slip in.
There is no wind. The pinkfoots' music swells.

You, you, you, you, you – they count,
and me. Strident, dissonant, unstinting.
They flock on the shore in thousands.

I look at the loch's smooth eye in their midst
and all the way to the city, as headlights scour
our gaze and motorway packs our ears, I think of it

and of what the geese, grown quiet, can hear:
swill of the water, stir in the willow scrub, the shift
of sheep on their feet in the moonless night.

Spate

The weather-teller pinecones have been closed for weeks.
   Nights, the sluice-drains ring with rain.
Days, the houses warp and steam, like deck strakes.

Look for the river – you'll reach it early: it's over-reached itself.
   It has new parts, distended margins
to a high mid-stream that plunges like a barn-loosed calf.

Not one canoeist, truant, summer swimmer touches it:
   bare winter water faces bristling cloud.
Listen – the drumroll showers deepen their ricochet.

And now every muscle of current knits to crisis;
   each flex, each spasm flows at triple speed:
the full river rushes to lose itself on fuller seas.

   And now an answering friction lifts: a line of geese
like a lever, prises a path upstream, flying the river
   inland, as they always have, tracing its ore to their roosts.

Some things starlings are sensitive to:

each other

wind

cloud shadows

hay bales

Kestrel

people-pass

grubs

each other

stubble-feel

tractor-sound

seeds

wires

worms

rooks

each other …

and so starling flocks are never still
but blow all day like the fields' leaves.

Blue hour

I walk out along the very line of land
    along the very keel of wind

        and through the stubble, flocks of grazing geese
        and on the shore, waders pick their feasts.

The west is cloud-in-pieces, sky-opera, inflamed,
the east is dim, even, opaque, gives nothing away

        and at times, a peregrine crosses latticely between
        and at times, the path unwinding hangs frail as a wire
                sure as a stile between.

Viscous, livid, the last sun melts across the fields.
Sudden, twice-size, a red moon floats over the sea

  and by illusion, I can stretch my arms and seem to touch them both
  and by eluding me, they seem, like gods, to talk above my head

        while what's fright, what's confidence
        what's loss, what's laughingness

        lie, as in a pan balance, still
        attended by the feeding of birds—

Till the minutes suck the light away
and the moon climbs grades of sapphire

and I turn and my step in the wind-drop quiet
is a thread to tack night
            to night.

Acknowledgements

Geraldine Clarkson

'Camelament' and 'When we awake' were previously published in *Under the Radar*. 'Love Cow' was previously commended in the *Poetry London* competition and published in *The Poetry Review* and 'a young woman undressed me and' has appeared in *Magma 64*. Geraldine Clarkson gratefully acknowledges the support of Arts Council England with her continued professional development.

Maureen Cullen

'Owl' was previously published in *Prole*, Issue 16. 'Apprentice' was published in *Reach Poetry*, issue 201. 'Dreaming Mum' and 'The Thin Place' were both published in *The Lake* webzine, June 2015.

Katie Griffiths

The poem 'Words for Sorrow' appeared in a previous version on the poet's own blog (A Woman in Goggles writes at http://thegriffithsmanoeuvre.blogspot.co.uk/) as 'Ten Words for Sorrow'.

Lucy Ingrams

'Stonechat's Song' appeared in *Magma 46* and 'Snow Tide' appeared in *Magma 55* (placed second in the *Magma* Poetry Competition, 2012). 'June' appeared in *Poetry Ireland Review 115* under the title 'Today,'. 'Slow Air' appeared in *New Writing Scotland 34*. 'Signs', 'A Hearting Space', 'So Will There Be Apples?' and 'August Letter' were published online as part of a portfolio of winning poems for the Manchester Poetry Prize, 2015.

Nine Arches Press would like to thank Ollie Dawson, Julia Bird and The Poetry School for all their support and enthusiasm which has helped to make Primers and *Primers: Volume One* possible. Many thanks are also due to Kathryn Maris, whose dedication and insight was invaluable in selecting, editing and mentoring the first four Primers poets.

Thank you to all the poets who entered the inaugural Primers scheme in 2015, and to those who were longlisted and those who were shortlisted. It was a pleasure to consider your work, and we wish all of you the very best with your writing in the future.